# Tall
## and Tiny

Retold by Jeanne Willis

Series Advisor Professor Kimberley Reynolds

Illustrated by Nicolás Aznárez

OXFORD
UNIVERSITY PRESS

# Letter from the Author

I have been writing stories since I was five and my Little Big Sister drew the pictures for them. I call her my Little Big Sister because although she is a year older than me, she is much shorter.

I feel like a giant when I stand next to her. That's why I have written two stories about a tall person and a tiny one.

Giants and little people often feature in old folk tales. *The Giant of Mont Saint-Michel* and *Tom Thumb* are set in the time of King Arthur. Read on and you will see that even if you are no bigger than a thumb, you can still stand up to the giant – just don't tell my sister!

*Jeanne Willis*

# The Giant of Mont Saint-Michel

**O**n the island of Mont Saint-Michel, there lived a giant.

He had legs like tree trunks ... fists like rocks ... and a wicked heart.

The giant lived all alone, but he wanted to be like other men. So he went to find a wife.

His footsteps shook the earth:

# BOOM! CRASH!

He crushed the villagers like ants.

He found Helena, who was the daughter of a duke.

He grabbed her in his huge fist.

'Wife!' he roared.

The giant took
Helena back to
his island.

Some knights sailed
over the sea to save her.
But the giant hit their
boat with rocks and
it sank.

The duke went to see King Arthur.
'Please save my daughter!' he begged.

So that night, the King and his men sailed to the island of Mont Saint-Michel.

King Arthur and his men marched into a dark wood.

In the wood they heard someone crying. It was an old woman. 'Go home!' she wailed. 'Go home or the giant will crush your bones.'

'I will kill the giant or die trying,' said Arthur. 'March on, men!'

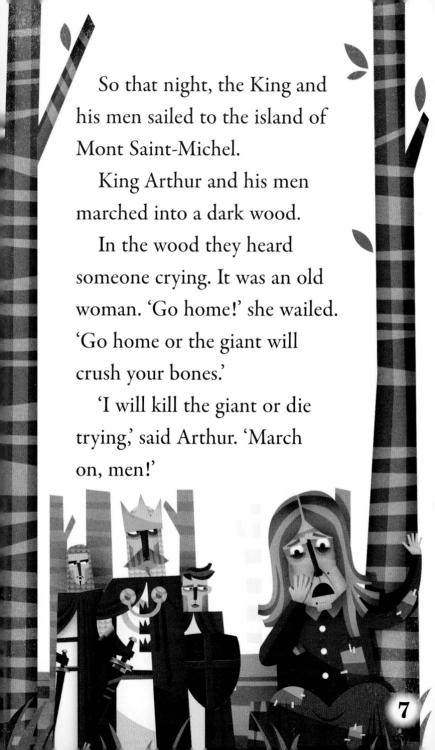

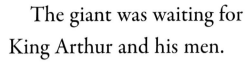

The giant was waiting for
King Arthur and his men.

The King waved his sword and cut
the giant's forehead.

The giant picked up his club.

He swung it so hard, the wind
blew King Arthur off his feet.

'Oh no!' said his men. 'The King
is no match for the giant!'

9

Then the cut on the giant's forehead began to bleed. Blood went into his eyes so he could not see.

King Arthur thrust his sword into the giant's heart, and he fell.

**BOOM!**
**CRASH!**

King Arthur rescued Helena and took her back to the duke's castle. 'The giant is dead!' he said.

'Good always wins in the end,' said the duke. 'Long live Good King Arthur!'

# Tom Thumb

In the days of King Arthur, there was a magician called Merlin.

Once, he went travelling dressed as a beggar. Along the way, he saw a farmer and begged him for food.

The farmer and his wife gave Merlin milk and bread. They were good to him, but they looked unhappy.

'Why are you so sad?' asked Merlin.

'We have no children,' said the farmer.

'I would love a son, even if he was no bigger than my thumb,' said his wife.

Merlin granted her wish.

Soon after, the farmer's wife had a son. He was so tiny that they called him Tom Thumb.

Tom Thumb was little, but he got into big trouble. When the farmer's wife made a cake, he fell into the mixture.

She did not see him there, and almost cooked him!

One day, a raven flew off with Tom Thumb.

It dropped him in the sea and a big fish chased him.

Tom tried to swim away, but the fish swallowed him in one gulp!

'Hey ho, it's very dark in here,' said Tom. 'Never mind. I will have a nap.'

The fish was caught and taken to the
castle. When the cook cut it open, out
came Tom!

'Goodness! This boy is no bigger than
my thumb!' said King Arthur.

He gave Tom his own little chair ...
his own little palace ... and his own little
coach pulled by six mice!

But the Queen was jealous of
Tom Thumb. She was so mean, Tom
hid from her in a snail shell.

Then a butterfly flew by. Tom Thumb
jumped on its back.

The Queen's knights
chased the butterfly.

At last, Tom fell off and they
caught him.

'Cut off his head!' said the Queen.

'Not now, dear,' said King Arthur.

'Do it tomorrow then!' she said.

Poor Tom was
put in a mousetrap.

In the night, a cat came. The cat thought
Tom was a mouse and broke the trap.

Tom fed the cat the
cheese from the trap
and was free!
He did a dance of joy
round the castle ballroom.

When the Queen saw him jigging about, she laughed out loud. 'Tom Thumb! However did you get free?' she said.

'I kept my head, Your Majesty!' he said.

He was so funny and brave and clever, the Queen forgave him.

Tom Thumb lived in his little palace for the rest of his days.

Not many people could make the Queen laugh, but he did. If the Queen was happy, King Arthur was happy.

Tom Thumb may have been little, but he had a great big smile.

Which is why everyone in the kingdom loved him **enormously**!